W0246790

THE LITTLE BOOK OF

REBEL WOMEN

First published in 2025 by OH
An Imprint of HEADLINE PUBLISHING GROUP LIMITED

2

Disclaimer:
All trademarks, copyright, quotations, company names, registered names, products, characters, logos and catchphrases used or cited in this book are the property of their respective owners.

Cataloguing in Publication Data is available from the British Library

ISBN 978-1-03542-237-1

Compiled and written by: Stella Caldwell
Editorial: Saneaah Muhammad
Designed and typeset in Avenir by: Andy Jones
Project manager: Russell Porter
Production: Rachel Burgess
Printed and bound in Dubai

Headline's policy is to use papers that are natural, renewable and recyclable products and made from wood grown in well-managed forests and other controlled sources. The logging and manufacturing processes are expected to conform to the environmental regulations of the country of origin.

HEADLINE PUBLISHING GROUP LIMITED
An Hachette UK Company
Carmelite House, 50 Victoria Embankment, London EC4Y 0DZ

The authorised representative in the EEA is Hachette Ireland, 8 Castlecourt Centre, Dublin 15, D15 XTP3, Ireland (email: info@hbgi.ie)

www.headline.co.uk www.hachette.co.uk

THE LITTLE BOOK OF

REBEL WOMEN

VOICES OF
COURAGE AND RESILIENCE

CONTENTS

INTRODUCTION

Throughout history, the world has been shaped by the indomitable spirit of women who have refused to conform to societal expectations. These figures, from diverse backgrounds and fields, have left indelible marks on society – they are the rebel women who have broken barriers and inspired countless others to follow in their footsteps.

In the realm of early feminist thought, philosopher and writer Mary Wollstonecraft stands as a towering figure. Her seminal work, *A Vindication of the Rights of Woman*, paved the way for future generations of women to demand their rights – women such as the suffragettes, who in the nineteenth and early-twentieth centuries fought fiercely and tirelessly for the right of women to vote.

Then there are figures – such as Sojourner Truth, a former slave turned abolitionist, or Malala Yousafzai, the Pakistani schoolgirl who defied the Taliban to champion girls' education – who exemplify the power of resilience and advocacy. Their words remind us that the fight for justice and equality is a timeless and universal struggle.

Art and literature have long been domains in which women have expressed their defiance and creativity. From Frida Kahlo's unapologetic self-portraits to the feisty heroines of Jane Austen or the poignant narratives of Maya Angelou, women in the arts have pushed boundaries and challenged societal norms.

In science, women such as Marie Curie, who won Nobel Prizes in both Physics and Chemistry, have made groundbreaking contributions, while in sport, politics and the business world, trailblazers have shattered glass ceilings and demonstrated that they can lead with vision and strength.

From the tenacious words of early pioneers to life-affirming advice from modern-day go-getters, this little book is a testament to the enduring impact of those women who have shaped our world. Their spirited voices urge us to embrace our own potential for change – and to continue the fight for a more just and equitable society.

CHAPTER ONE

PIONEERS OF CHANGE

Throughout history, remarkable women have stood boldly against the tide of societal expectations and limitations.

From Elizabeth I, the most powerful woman of her time, to the brave suffragettes who secured the right to vote, these trailblazers defied convention and laid the foundations for progress.

> “I will not be triumphed over.”

Queen Cleopatra VII
The last pharaoh of Egypt

I know I have the body of a weak and feeble woman; but I have the heart and stomach of a king – and of a king of England too.

”

Queen Elizabeth I
Speech to her troops at Tilbury, 1588

I wish to persuade women to endeavour to acquire strength, both of mind and body, and to convince them that the soft phrases, susceptibility of heart, delicacy of sentiment and refinement of taste, are almost synonymous with epithets of weakness, and that those beings are only the objects of pity, and that kind of love which has been termed its sister, will soon become objects of contempt.

Mary Wollstonecraft

British writer and philosopher, *A Vindication of the Rights of Woman*, 1792

I do not wish [women] to have power over men; but over themselves.

”

Mary Wollstonecraft

British writer and philosopher, *A Vindication of the Rights of Woman*, 1792

I know nothing of man's rights, or woman's rights; human rights are all that I recognize.

”

Sarah Moore Grimké

American abolitionist and campaigner for women's rights, *Letters on the Equality of the Sexes, and the Condition of Women*, 1838

We have waited here long in the dust; we are tired and hungry; but the triumphal procession must appear at last.

”

Margaret Fuller
American journalist, editor, critic, translator and women's rights advocate, *Woman in the Nineteenth Century*, 1845

If the first woman God ever made was strong enough to turn the world upside down all alone, these women together ought to be able to turn it back, and get it right side up again!

”

Sojourner Truth

American campaigner for abolition and civil and women's rights, in a speech delivered at the Ohio Women's Rights Convention, 1851

Any great change must expect opposition, because it shakes the very foundation of privilege.

Lucretia Mott

American abolitionist and women's rights campaigner, in a speech at the Women's Rights Convention in Seneca Falls, 1848

Woman is learning for herself that not self-sacrifice, but self-development, is her first duty in life; and this, not primarily for the sake of others but that she may become fully herself.

Matilda Joslyn Gage

American writer and activist,
Woman, Church and State, 1893

Life is not easy for any of us. But what of that? We must have perseverance and above all confidence in ourselves. We must believe that we are gifted for something and that this thing must be attained. ”

Marie Curie

Polish-French physicist and chemist who won the 1903 Nobel Prize in Physics and the 1911 Nobel Prize in Chemistry

It is probably true to say that the largest scope for change still lies in men's attitude to women, and in women's attitude to themselves.

Vera Brittain

British Red Cross nurse during the First World War who became a writer and pacifist

You have to make more noise than anybody else, you have to make yourself more obtrusive than anybody else, you have to fill all the papers more than anybody else, in fact you have to be there all the time and see that they do not snow you under, if you are really going to get your reform realized.

Emmeline Pankhurst

Leader of the British suffragette movement, in a speech delivered in 1913

Remember the dignity of your womanhood. Do not appeal, do not beg, do not grovel. Take courage, join hands, stand besides us, fight with us.

”

Christabel Pankhurst

British suffragette who co-founded the Women's Social and Political Union in 1903

Women's freedom is the sign of social freedom.

Rosa Luxemburg

Polish-German revolutionary socialist and anti-war activist during the First World War, and fierce champion of women's rights

The true militant suffragette is an epitome of the determination of women to possess their own souls. ”

Emily Wilding Davison

British suffragette who died after jumping in front of King George V's horse at the 1913 Derby

I may be the first woman member of Congress, but I won't be the last.

”

Jeannette Rankin

American politician who, in 1916, became the first woman to hold federal office in the United States

Stand for something or you will fall for anything. Today's mighty oak is yesterday's nut that held its ground.

”

Rosa Parks

African-American activist, known as the "First Lady of Civil Rights" for her role in the Montgomery Bus Boycott, after she refused to give up her bus seat to a white man in 1955

Each suburban wife struggled with it alone. As she made the beds, shopped for groceries, matched slipcover material, ate peanut butter sandwiches with her children, chauffeured Cub Scouts and Brownies, lay beside her husband at night – she was afraid to ask even of herself the silent question – 'Is this all?' ❞

Betty Friedan
American feminist writer and activist,
The Feminine Mystique, 1963

The woman power of this nation can be the power which makes us whole and heals the rotten community, now so shattered by war and poverty and racism. I have great faith in the power of women who will dedicate themselves whole-heartedly to the task of remaking our society. ”

Coretta Scott King

American author, civil rights leader and the wife of Martin Luther King Jr, in a speech delivered three weeks after the death of her husband, 1968

We cannot expect in the immediate future that all women who seek it will achieve full equality of opportunity. But if women are to start moving towards that goal, we must believe in ourselves or no one else will believe in us; we must match our aspirations with the competence, courage and determination to succeed. ”

Rosalyn Yalow

American medical physicist and co-winner of the 1977 Nobel Prize in Physiology or Medicine

CHAPTER TWO

COURAGE AND DEFIANCE

Challenging the status quo takes courage. This chapter celebrates the bravery and defiance of women who refused to be silenced.

Exposing injustice and fighting for their beliefs, their fearless actions and bold voices have ignited change and inspired countless others to follow their example.

One life is all we have and we live it as we believe in living it. But to sacrifice what you are and to live without belief, that is a fate more terrible than dying.

Joan of Arc
Patron saint of France

The best protection a woman can have... is courage.

”

Elizabeth Cady Stanton
American writer, activist and suffragist, at the Women's Rights Convention in Seneca Falls, 1848

Life is either a daring adventure or nothing.

Helen Keller

American author, disability rights advocate, political activist and lecturer, *Let Us Have Faith*, 1940

At the end of the day, we can endure much more than we think we can.

Frida Kahlo

Mexican painter, renowned for being the first female artist to rebel against the rules of art to explore themes of identity and feminism

“I know what I want, I have a goal, I have opinions, a religion and love. If only I can be myself, I’ll be satisfied. I know that I’m a woman, a woman with inner strength and a great deal of courage!”

Anne Frank
The Diary of a Young Girl, 1947

You gain strength, courage and confidence by every experience in which you really stop to look fear in the face. You are able to say to yourself, 'I have lived through this horror. I can take the next thing that comes along.' You must do the thing you think you cannot do.

”

Eleanor Roosevelt
Former First Lady of the United States, diplomat and activist

The most courageous act is still to think for yourself. Aloud.

Coco Chanel
French fashion designer and businesswoman

Women, if the soul of the nation is to be saved, I believe you must become its soul.

”

Coretta Scott King
American author, civil rights leader, and the wife of Martin Luther King Jr

"I'll tell you what freedom is to me: no fear. I mean really, no fear!"

Nina Simone
American singer-songwriter, pianist and civil rights activist

I've been absolutely terrified every minute of my life – and I've never let it keep me from doing a single thing I wanted to do.

”

Georgia O'Keeffe

American painter, famous for her radical and fascinating depiction of flowers that evoke themes of feminity and sexuality

"

Life shrinks or expands in proportion to one's courage.

"

Anaïs Nin

French-born American diarist, essayist and novelist, famed for being one of the first women to explore the realm of erotic writing

No one ever became a success without taking chances. One must be able to recognize the moment and seize it without delay.

”

Estée Lauder
American businesswoman

Courage is like a muscle. We strengthen it with use.

”

Ruth Gordon

American actress, playwright and screenwriter

Think like a queen. A queen is not afraid to fail. Failure is another stepping stone to greatness.

Oprah Winfrey

American talk show host, television producer, author and actress

We need women who are so strong they can be gentle, so educated they can be humble, so fierce they can be compassionate, so passionate they can be rational, and so disciplined they can be free.

Kavita Ramdas

American feminist and activist, and former president and CEO of the Global Fund for Women

I am a woman.
Phenomenally.
Phenomenal woman.
That's me.

”

Maya Angelou
American poet and civil rights activist,
"Phenomenal Woman", *And Still I Rise*, 1978

Though we tremble before uncertain futures may we meet illness, death and adversity with strength, may we dance in the face of our fears.

Gloria Anzaldúa

American author and poet, and scholar of Chicana feminism, cultural theory and queer theory

The connections between and among women are the most feared, the most problematic and the most potentially transforming force on the planet. ”

Adrienne Rich
American poet, essayist and feminist

I am too intelligent, too demanding and too resourceful for anyone to be able to take charge of me entirely. No one knows me or loves me completely. I have only myself.

”

Simone de Beauvoir

French existentialist philosopher, social theorist, writer and feminist activist, known for her trailblazing work in feminist philosophy

I tell young people: Do not think of yourself, think of others. Think of the future that awaits you, think about what you can do and do not fear anything.

Rita Levi-Montalcini
Italian neurologist and 1986 Nobel Prize co-winner in Physiology or Medicine

I have chosen to no longer be apologetic for my femaleness and my femininity. And I want to be respected in all of my femaleness because I deserve to be.

Chimamanda Ngozi Adichie
Nigerian writer and public speaker, renowned for her literature surrounding postcolonial feminism

There are so many people out there who will tell you that you can't. What you've got to do is turn around and say, 'Watch me'.

Layne Beachley
Australian former professional surfer and seven-time World Champion winner

To me, 'fearless' is not the absence of fear. It's not being completely unafraid. To me, fearless is having fears. Fearless is having doubts. Lots of them. To me, fearless is living in spite of those things that scare you to death.

Taylor Swift
American singer-songwriter

"Am I good enough?
Yes, I am."

Michelle Obama
American attorney, author and former First Lady of the United States, *Becoming*, 2018

When I'm hungry, I eat. When I'm thirsty, I drink. When I feel like saying something, I say it.

Madonna
American singer-songwriter and actress

I'm my own woman. Nobody can tell me what I can and cannot do.

”

Amna Al Haddad
Emirati weightlifting athlete and former journalist

CHAPTER THREE

RABBLE ROUSERS

Across the decades, fearless agitators have boldly stirred the pot.

Challenging complacency and igniting movements, their provocative actions and outspoken rhetoric have sparked debates and galvanized supporters.

Through their powerful words, we glimpse their struggles, triumphs and indomitable spirit.

Every great dream begins with a dreamer. Always remember, you have within you the strength, the patience and the passion to reach for the stars to change the world. ”

Harriet Tubman
American abolitionist and suffragist who escaped slavery in 1849

The young women of today, free to study, to speak, to write, to choose their occupation, should remember that every inch of this freedom was bought for them at a great price. It is for them to show their gratitude by helping onward the reforms of their own times, by spreading the light of freedom and of truth still wider. The debt that each generation owes to the past it must pay to the future.

Abigail Scott Duniway

American newspaper editor, writer and prominent suffragist

There shall never be another season of silence until women have the same rights men have on this green earth.

Susan B. Anthony

American social reformer and suffragist, after being arrested and fined for casting a vote in the 1872 United States presidential election (in violation of laws that allowed only men to vote)

Courage calls to courage everywhere, and its voice cannot be denied.

”

Millicent Fawcett

English women's rights campaigner, writer and former leader of the National Union of Women's Suffrage Societies

Do not be afraid to fight for what is right, even in the face of adversity.

Dolores Ibárruri, "La Pasionaria"

Spanish Republican politician of the Spanish Civil War and co-founder of World Committee of Women Against War and Fascism

Women, like men, should try to do the impossible. ”

Amelia Earhart

American aviation pioneer who, in 1937, became the first female aviator to attempt to circumnavigate the globe. She disappeared over the Pacific Ocean.

The best way for us to cultivate fearlessness in our daughters and other young women is by example. If they see their mothers and other women in their lives going forward despite fear, they'll know it's possible.

Gloria Steinem

American journalist and a key figure in the Women's Liberation Movement

I am not free while any woman is unfree, even when her shackles are very different from my own.

”

Audre Lorde

American writer, intersectional feminist, poet and civil rights activist, during a presentation at the National Women's Studies Association Conference, Connecticut, June 1981

The question isn't who is going to let me; it's who is going to stop me.

Ayn Rand
Russian-American author and philosopher

Certain people – men, of course – discouraged me, saying [science] was not a good career for women. That pushed me even more to persevere.

Françoise Barré-Sinoussi

French virologist who discovered the HIV virus that causes AIDS, and who was the co-winner of the 2008 Nobel Prize in Physiology or Medicine

When a woman rises up in glory, her energy is magnetic and her sense of possibility contagious.

Marianne Williamson
American author, speaker and political activist,
A Woman's Worth, 2003

I can promise you that women working together – linked, informed and educated – can bring peace and prosperity to this forsaken planet. ”

Isabel Allende

Chilean-American writer and human rights activist

If they refuse to make space for you at the table, then create your own table.

”

Graça Machel
Mozambician politician and humanitarian

I raise up my voice – not so that I can shout, but so that those without a voice can be heard... We cannot all succeed when half of us are held back.

”

Malala Yousafzai

Pakistani female education activist and 2014 Nobel Peace Prize laureate, during a speech at the United Nations, 12 July 2013

Fight for the things that you care about, but do it in a way that will lead others to join you.

Ruth Bader Ginsburg

American lawyer, jurist, first female professor at Columbia Law School and co-founder of the Women's Rights Project at the American Civil Liberties Union

It actually doesn't take much to be considered a difficult woman. That's why there are so many of us.

”

Jane Goodall
British zoologist, primatologist and anthropologist

Each time a woman stands up for herself, without knowing it possibly, without claiming it, she stands up for all women.

”

Maya Angelou
American poet and civil rights activist

Women belong in all places where decisions are being made. It shouldn't be that women are the exception.

”

Ruth Bader Ginsburg

American lawyer, jurist, first female professor at Columbia Law School and co-founder of the Women's Rights Project at the American Civil Liberties Union

No country can ever truly flourish if it stifles the potential of its women and deprives itself of the contributions of half of its citizens.

”

Michelle Obama

American attorney, author and former First Lady of the United States

When you grow up as a girl, it is like there are faint chalk lines traced approximately three inches around your entire body at all times, drawn by society and often religion and family and particularly other women, who somehow feel invested in how you behave, as if your actions reflect directly on all womanhood. ”

M.E. Thomas

Confessions of a Sociopath: A Life Spent Hiding in Plain Sight, 2013

I want all the girls without an exception to have that space for themselves where they have opportunities to be the women they wish to be. ”

Priyanka Chopra
Indian actress and film producer

My mother did not raise me to ask for permission to lead. ”

Ayanna Pressley
American congresswoman

There are two powers in the world; one is the sword and the other is the pen. There is a third power stronger than both, that of women.

Malala Yousafzai

Pakistani female education activist and 2014 Nobel Peace Prize laureate, *I Am Malala: The Girl Who Stood Up for Education and Was Shot by the Taliban*, 2012

When the witch hunters imprisoned our ancestors when they tried to burn the magic away. Someone should have warned them that magic cannot be tamed. Because you cannot burn away what has always been aflame.

Nikita Gill

Irish-Indian poet, playwright, writer and illustrator, "Dragon's Breath", *Wild Embers: Poems of Rebellion, Fire and Beauty*, 2017.

CHAPTER FOUR

BREAKING BARRIERS

Across the decades, pioneering women have blazed a trail in their respective fields and achived incredible firsts.

From politics to the arts, and from science to sports, these groundbreakers have proved that excellence knows no bounds – and have paved the way for future generations to rise and thrive.

I am satisfied that if a book is a good one, it is so whatever the sex of the author may be.

”

Anne Brontë
English novelist and poet, *The Tenant of Wildfell Hall*, 1848

I have had a larger responsibility of human lives than ever man or woman had before. And I attribute my success to this – I never gave or took an excuse.

”

Florence Nightingale
English social reformer, statistician and the founder of modern nursing

The horrors and disgusts I have no doubt of vanquishing. I have overcome stronger distastes than any that now remain and feel fully equal to the contest. As to the opinion of people, I don't care one straw personally...

Elizabeth Blackwell

English-American physician who, in 1849, became the first woman to graduate from medical school in the United States

Let me tell you what I think of bicycling. I think it has done more to emancipate women than anything else in the world… I stand and rejoice every time I see a woman ride by on a wheel… The moment she takes her seat, she knows she can't get into harm unless she gets off her bicycle, and away she goes, the picture of free, untrammelled womanhood.

Susan B. Anthony

American social reformer and suffragist, in an interview with journalist Nelly Bly in 1896

I refused to take no for an answer.

”

Bessie Coleman

The first African-American woman and first Native American to earn an international pilot's license, in 1921

You create opportunities by performing, not complaining. ”

Muriel Siebert

American businesswoman and the first female member of the New York Stock Exchange, in 1967

It's so nice to be a spoke in the wheel, one that helps to turn, not one that hinders.

Gertrude Bell

English writer, traveller, political officer and archaeologist, and the first western woman to map and travel solo across Arabia

I was a liberated woman long before there was a name for it.

”

Peggy Guggenheim
American art collector and socialite

Girls are capable of doing everything men are capable of doing. Sometimes they have more imagination than men.

”

Katherine Johnson

American mathematician, one of the first African-American women to work as a NASA scientist, and recipient of the Presidential Medal of Freedom in 2015

Just don't give up trying to do what you really want to do. Where there is love and inspiration, I don't think you can go wrong.

Ella Fitzgerald
American jazz singer

"This land, my sister, is a woman."

Fadwa Tuqan

The first Palestinian woman to dedicate her life to writing poetry

Technique and ability alone do not get you to the top; it is the willpower that is most important.

”

Junko Tabei

Japanese mountaineer and author who, in 1975, because the first woman to reach the summit of Mount Everest

To be liberated, woman must feel free to be herself, not in rivalry to man but in the context of her own capacity and her personality.

”

Indira Gandhi

Indian politician and stateswoman who, in 1966, became the first female prime minister of India

If they don't give you a seat at the table, bring a folding chair.

”

Shirley Chisholm

American politician who, in 1968, became the first African-American woman to be elected to the United States Congress

Champions keep playing until they get it right.

Billie Jean King
American former world No.1 tennis player and winner of 39 Grand Slam tennis titles

Tremendous amounts of talent are being lost to our society just because that talent wears a skirt.

Shirley Chisholm

American politician who, in 1968, became the first African-American woman to be elected to the United States Congress

In politics, if you want anything said, ask a man. If you want anything done, ask a woman.

Margaret Thatcher

British politican and the first female prime minister of Britain, in a speech addressing a women's group in 1965

I believe that fortitude is key. More than anything, be consistent. Go at it. Go at it. Go at it. When you succeed, don't forget the responsibility of making somebody else succeed with you.

Antonia Novello

Puerto Rican physician who, in 1990, became the first female and first Hispanic United States Surgeon General

Think big. That's what I have always been encouraged to do and it works. Throughout my life, I've been taught that anything is possible... If you think massive, then you will get further than if you think realistic.

Martha Lane Fox
British businesswoman, philanthropist and public servant

I think for girls it's really important to show them that it is possible to dream big, and if your dreams include some nerdy creation, that's fine. ”

Juliana Rotich
Kenyan information technologist and entrepreneur

As women achieve power, the barriers will fall.

Sandra Day O'Connor

American attorney, politician and the first woman to serve as a United States Supreme Court justice

It took me quite a long time to develop a voice, and now that I have it, I am not going to be silent.

”

Madeleine Albright
American diplomat, political scientist and the first woman to become the United States Secretary of State

You could certainly say that I've never underestimated myself. There's nothing wrong with being ambitious. ”

Angela Merkel

Former German politician and the first female Chancellor of her country

I think, if the world can be saved, it will be by women. ”

Vigdís Finnbogadóttir

Former Icelandic president, and the world's first democratically elected female president

Women are leaders everywhere you look – from the CEO who runs a Fortune 500 company to the housewife who raises her children and heads her household. Our country was built by strong women, and we will continue to break down walls and defy stereotypes.

Nancy Pelosi

American politician and the first woman to be elected as United States House Speaker

I've gone through the glass ceiling, and that's an important message to send to young women and girls... 'Yes, it's possible if you are a woman.'

Ameenah Gurib-Fakim

Mauritian biodiversity scientist, politician and the first female president of Mauritius

We need women at all levels, including the top, to change the dynamic, reshape the conversation, to make sure women's voices are heard and heeded, not overlooked and ignored.

Sheryl Sandberg

American technology executive and former chief operating officer of Facebook

It has taken 232 years and 115 prior appointments for a Black woman to be selected to serve on the Supreme Court of the United States, but we've made it! We've made it – all of us.

Ketanji Brown Jackson
American lawyer, jurist and the first Black woman to serve on the Supreme Court

One of the criticisms I've faced over the years is that I'm not aggressive enough or assertive enough, or maybe somehow, because I'm empathetic, it means I'm weak. I totally rebel against that. I refuse to believe that you cannot be both compassionate and strong.

”

Jacinda Ardern

Former New Zealand politician and the country's first female prime minister

You have to believe in yourself when no one else does.

Serena Williams

American tennis player and 23-time Grand Slam champion, addressing the graduating class of 2020 at Mouratoglou Tennis Academy

What I want young women and girls to know is: You are powerful and your voice matters.

Kamala Harris

The first woman and woman of colour to be elected as United States vice president and certified as a presidential nominee

Ignore the glass ceiling and do your work. If you're focusing on the glass ceiling, focusing on what you don't have, focusing on the limitations, then you will be limited. ”

Ava DuVernay
American filmmaker, screenwriter and producer

CHAPTER FIVE

HEROINES OF WORD AND SCREEN

As society has evolved, so too has the role of women in literature and on screen. This chapter celebrates the strong female characters who have captivated readers and audiences.

Showing courage and intelligence, these heroines have defied stereotypes and left an indelible mark on our cultural landscape.

Do you not know I am a woman? When I think, I must speak.

”

Rosalind

As You Like It, William Shakespeare,
Act 3, Scene 2

“If I be waspish, best beware my sting.”

Katherine
The Taming of the Shew, William Shakespeare,
Act 2, Scene 1

There is a stubbornness about me that can never bear to be frightened at the will of others. My courage always rises at every attempt to intimidate me.

”

Elizabeth Bennet

Pride and Prejudice, Jane Austen, 1813

“I hate to hear you talk about all women as if they were fine ladies instead of rational creatures. None of us want to be in calm waters all our lives.”

Mrs Croft

Persuasion, Jane Austen, 1817

I am no bird; and no net ensnares me; I am a free human being with an independent will.

”

Jane Eyre
Jane Eyre, Charlotte Brontë, 1847

I shall be up before you are awake; I shall be afield before you are up; and I shall have breakfasted before you are afield. In short, I shall astonish you all.

”

Bathsheba Everdene
Far From the Madding Crowd,
Thomas Hardy, 1874

I am not afraid of storms, for I am learning how to sail my ship.

Amy March
Little Women, Louisa May Alcott, 1868–1869

Oh, it's delightful to have ambitions. I'm so glad I have such a lot. And there never seems to be any end to them – that's the best of it. Just as soon as you attain to one ambition you see another one glittering higher up still. It does make life so interesting.

Anne Shirley

Anne of Green Gables, L. M. Montgomery, 1908

'Whatever comes,' she said, 'cannot alter one thing. If I am a princess in rags and tatters, I can be a princess inside. It would be easy to be a princess if I were dressed in cloth of gold, but it is a great deal more of a triumph to be one all the time when no one knows it.'

Sara Crewe

A Little Princess, Frances Hodgson Burnett, 1905

A woman knows very well that, though a wit sends her his poems, praises her judgement, solicits her criticism, and drinks her tea, this by no means signifies that he respects her opinions, admires her understanding, or will refuse, though the rapier is denied him, to run through the body with his pen.

Virginia Woolf
Orlando, 1928

Don't you worry about me. I'll always come out on top.

Astrid Lindgren
Pippi Longstocking, 1945

Never do anything by halves if you want to get away with it. Be outrageous. Go the whole hog. Make sure everything you do is so completely crazy it's unbelievable...

”

Matilda

Matilda, Roald Dahl, 1988

Nolite Te Bastardes Carborundorum.
Don't let the bastards grind you down.

”

June/Offred
The Handmaid's Tale, Margaret Atwood, 1985

Okay, she's tough, but if Miranda were a man…no one would notice anything about her, except how great she is at her job.

”

Lauren Weisberger
The Devil Wears Prada, 2003

She'd decided long ago that life was a long journey. She would be strong and she would be weak, and both would be okay.

”

Tahereh Mafi
Furthermore, 2016

I am a woman and a warrior. If you think I can't be both, you've been lied to.

Jennifer Zeynab Joukhadar
The Map of Salt and Stars, 2018

As God is my witness, as God is my witness they're not going to lick me. I'm going to live through this and when it's all over, I'll never be hungry again. No, nor any of my folk. If I have to lie, steal cheat or kill. As God is my witness, I'll never be hungry again.

Scarlett O'Hara
Gone with the Wind, 1936

“I want to be alone.”

Grusinskaya
(played by Greta Garbo)
Grand Hotel, 1932

“

I am big. It’s the pictures that got small.

”

Norma Desmond

Sunset Boulevard, 1950.

You get what you settle for. ”

Louise Sawyer
Thelma and Louise, 1991

I'm a damsel. I'm in distress. I can handle this. Have a nice day!

Megara
Hercules, 1997.

Girls, come on. Leave the saving of the world to the men? I don't think so!

”

Elastigirl
The Incredibles, 2004

Have some fire.
Be unstoppable.
Be a force of nature.
Be better than anyone here and don't give a damn what anyone else thinks.

”

Dr Cristina Yang
Grey's Anatomy, 2005

I know how to run without you holding my hand! ”

Rey

Star Wars: The Force Awakens, 2015

Ever since I was a child, I felt like greatness was in store for me. Like God himself had spat me forth to land on this Earth and, in some way, transform it.

”

Catherine the Great
The Great, 2020

I didn't get anywhere in my life waiting on somebody's permission.

Shirley Chisholm
"Shirley", *Mrs America*, 2020

CHAPTER SIX

WIT AND WISDOM

Encapsulating strength and intelligence, the quotes on the following pages offer timeless guidance and inspiration.

From political leaders to trailblazing activists, and from Hollywood leading ladies to literary legends, each of these voices enriches our understanding of what it means to be strong and empowered.

The more I study, the more insatiable do I feel my genius for it to be.

Ada Lovelace

English mathematician and writer, and one of the world's first computer programmers

Women feel just as men feel; they need exercise for their faculties and a field for their efforts, as much as their brothers do; they suffer from too rigid a restraint… precisely as men would suffer; and it is narrow-minded… to say that they ought to confine themselves to making puddings and knitting stockings, to playing on the piano and embroidering bags. ”

Charlotte Brontë

English novelist and poet, *Jane Eyre*, 1847

Don't sit down and wait
for the opportunities to come...
get up and make them.

Madam C. J. Walker
(born Sarah Breedlove)
American businesswoman and the first female self-made millionaire in the United States

There is no gate, no lock, no bolt that you can set upon the freedom of my mind.

Virginia Woolf
English novelist and essayist,
A Room of One's Own, 1929

Many receive advice, only the wise profit from it.

Harper Lee

American novelist and winner of the 1961 Pulitzer Prize for her celebrated novel, *To Kill a Mockingbird* (1960), and winner of the United States Presidential Medal of Freedom in 2007

If you do what interests you, at least one person is pleased.

Katharine Hepburn
American actress and Hollywood legend

Feet, what do I need you for if I have wings to fly? ”

Frida Kahlo

Mexican painter, renowned for being the first female artist to rebel against the rules of art to explore themes of identity and feminism

Always be a first-rate version of yourself, instead of a second-rate version of somebody else.

Judy Garland
American actress, singer and dancer

I myself have never been able to find out precisely what feminism is: I only know that people call me a feminist whenever I express sentiments that differentiate me from a doormat.

Rebecca West

British author, journalist, literary critic and travel writer, *The Clarion*, 13 November 1913

People say, what is the sense of our small effort? They cannot see that we must lay one brick at a time. A pebble cast into a pond causes ripples that spread in all directions. Each one of our thoughts, words and deeds is like that. No one has a right to sit down and feel hopeless. There is too much work to do.

99

Dorothy Day

American journalist and social activist

A girl should be two things: who and what she wants.

Coco Chanel
French fashion designer and businesswoman

And the day came when the risk to remain tight in a bud was more painful than the risk it took to blossom.

Anaïs Nin

French-born American diarist, essayist and novelist, famed for being one of the first women to explore the realm of erotic writing

Power has to come from inside. It has to come from knowing who you are, why you're on earth, what is the meaning of your life. That's power. If it's all about armour, possessions and weapons, that's not power.

Jane Fonda
American actress and activist

As you grow older, you will discover that you have two hands, one for helping yourself, the other for helping others.

”

Audrey Hepburn
British actress and
UNICEF Goodwill Ambassador

The most common way people give up their power is by thinking they don't have any.

”

Alice Walker

American novelist, poet, social activist and the first African-American woman to win the Pulitzer Prize for Fiction, for her groundbreaking novel, *The Colour Purple* (1982)

Freeing yourself was one thing, claiming ownership of that freed self was another. ”

Toni Morrison

American novelist and editor, winner of the Pulitzer Prize for her novel *Beloved* (1987), winner of the Nobel Prize in Literature in 1993 and awarded with the Presidential Medal of Freedom in 2012

What's the greatest lesson a woman should learn? That since day one, she's already had everything she needs within herself. It's the world that convinced her she did not.

Rupi Kaur

Indian-Canadian poet, illustrator and author, *The Sun and Her Flowers*, 2017

And the moon said to me – my darling daughter, you do not have to be whole in order to shine.

”

Nichole McElhaney
American writer and poet

No woman gets an orgasm from shining the kitchen floor.

”

Betty Friedan

American feminist writer and activist. She was the author of *The Feminine Mystique* (1963), credited with sparking second-wave feminism in the United States.

We're all water from different rivers, that's why it's so easy to meet; we're all water in this vast, vast ocean, someday we'll evaporate together. ”

Yoko Ono
Japanese multi-media artist and peace activist

Women are not pals enough with men, so we must make ourselves indispensable. After all, we have the greatest weapon in our hands by just being women.

Maria Callas
American-Greek soprano

A woman with a voice is, by definition, a strong woman. ”

Melinda French Gates

American philanthropist, winner of the United States Presidential Medal of Freedom in 2016 and ranked as one of the world's most powerful women by *Forbes* magazine

Don't let a king or a prince or a fairytale tell you you are smaller than that or who you are meant to be.

99

Nikita Gill

Irish-Indian poet , playwright, writer and illustrator, "Dragon's Breath", *Wild Embers: Poems of Rebellion, Fire and Beauty*, 2017

I've never been interested in being invisible and erased.

Laverne Cox
American actress and activist

Love yourself first and everything else falls into line. ”

Lucille Ball

American actress, comedian and producer who, in 1962, became the first woman to run a major television studio

If you know you are on the right track, if you have this inner knowledge, then nobody can turn you off... no matter what they say.

Barbara McClintock

American scientist and cytogeneticist, and winner of the 1983 Nobel Prize in Physiology or Medicine

Well-behaved women seldom make history.

Laurel Thatcher Ulrich
American historian specializing in the history of women, and winner of the 1991 Pulitzer Prize in History

A woman without a man is like a fish without a bicycle.

Irina Dunn
Australian writer, social activist and filmmaker

They'll tell you you're too loud – that you need to wait your turn; and ask the right people for permission. Do it anyway.

Alexandria Ocasio-Cortez
American congresswoman

If you think you're too small to have an impact, try going to bed with a mosquito in the room.

”

Anita Roddick

British businesswoman and human rights activist, best known for founding The Body Shop

What you do makes a difference, and you have to decide what kind of difference you want to make.

”

Jane Goodall
British zoologist, primatologist and anthropologist

Courage, sacrifice, determination, commitment, toughness, heart, talent, guts. That's what little girls are made of; the heck with sugar and spice.

Bethany Hamilton
American professional surfer and writer,
Soul Surfer, 2004

Above all, be the heroine of your life, not the victim. ”

Nora Ephron
American journalist, writer and filmmaker

I'd rather regret the risks that didn't work out than the chances I didn't take at all. ”

Simone Biles

American gymnast and winner of 11 Olympic and 30 World Championship medals

“Find out who you are. And do it on purpose.”

Dolly Parton
American singer-songwriter,
actress, businesswoman and philantrophist

For I conclude that the enemy is not lipstick, but guilt itself; that we deserve lipstick, if we want it, AND free speech; we deserve to be sexual AND serious – or whatever we please; we are entitled to wear cowboy boots to our own revolution.

Naomi Wolf
American feminist author and journalist

There's something so special about a woman who dominates in a man's world. It takes a certain grace, strength, intelligence, fearlessness, and the nerve to never take no for an answer.

Rihanna
Barbadian singer and businesswoman

The only one who can tell you 'you can't win' is you, and you don't have to listen. ”

Jessica Ennis-Hill
Former British track and field athlete and Olympic gold medallist

I think women are scared of feeling powerful and strong and brave sometimes. There's nothing wrong with being afraid. It's not the absence of fear, it's overcoming it and sometimes you just have to blast through and have faith.

Emma Watson

British actress and activist, and a United Nations Women Goodwill Ambassador

Success is often about how you deal with failure. When something goes seriously wrong, you can either give up or you can dig deep, recover your self-belief and focus once more upon your goal. It's all about your attitude and being positive, even when everything sometimes seems stacked against you.

Tanni Grey-Thompson

Welsh Paralympic star, disability rights champion, television presenter and life peer

You could make a case that, along with the technological revolution, the most provocative upending destabilizing thrilling change in the course of human history is that we're finally in it. … We're here now, women are in the world, and we will not be bullied.

Meryl Streep

American actress, during the closing speech at the 2016 Women in the World Summit

We must open the doors and we must see to it they remain open, so that others can pass through. ”

Rosemary Brown
Canadian politician and the first Black woman elected to the provincial government of British Columbia

Any little girl who's practising her speech on the telly, you never know. I used to work as a cleaner and I loved that job, but I did spend quite a lot of my time imagining this. ”

Olivia Colman

British actress, during her Oscar acceptance speech at the 2019 Academy Awards

The reality is: sometimes you lose. And you're never too good to lose. You're never too big to lose. You're never too smart to lose. It happens.

Beyoncé Knowles-Carter

American singer-songwriter and businesswoman

Speak your truth, even if your voice shakes.

Maggie Kuhn

American activist and founder of the Gray Panthers Movement